CONTENTS

This book is not about religion. It is about real lives where love is needed and taken.

This book is about the life of Buddha - a real person who enlightened, found Buddhism - and was worshipped as the leader.

And with the desire to bring the understanding of the Buddha most naturally and gently like poems, the author wrote out the Buddha's life in the form of six-eight-poetry (a pair of basic verses consisting of a six-syllable sentence and an eight-syllable sentence rhyming together) - a simple, idyllic, emotional, easy-to-approach poetry form of the Vietnamese people.

Thanks much for your care!

I wish you all the best!

Sincerely!

A happy dream

In the Himalayas[1]
Clouds on peaks. Under, snow-bound
Hillside, a scene was found
Floating fog, getting down rainy

Old north India[2] could see
A nice place. A poetry kingdom
One day, a good happened
Made the world jubilant, whole changes

Maya[3]'s deep sleep - the Queen
Shiny dream of..., had been done, yet
Heaven lights with streams
Shimmered down, just, it filled her bed

In the halo, among
An elephant with six tusks appeared
It flew, by lights there
It made her melted! Immediately

Morning, she woke quickly
The Queen's full of joy. Be asked her...?
Told the King strange matters
Suddhodana[4]: "Officials, come here!"

Gathered all of, with dear
Guessed the dream fast, clear - helped King
All of them as singing:
"This event's good! This thing's no fear!

Happy news must be here
The Queen conceives, a year later
That's inevitable
Brilliant genius, future Prince

Will be born, help people
As a great member of life
For the King of Shakya[5]
For human - near, far - find sweetness!"

Lovely looked at the Queen
The King showed his meaning in mind
For a long time, desired
The son grows up - tries to the King

Twenty years of waiting
Reality gets. This thing comes true

Full moon in April, Buddha was born

As was said, of course, is
The Queen's pregnancy, once day
It was fun! That's great fun!
The wind went with incense fulfilled

Followed ancient Indians
"Own home give birth, return parents'"
There, the place of having
Blooming: peace! Custom obeyed

Knew the birth, near these days
Rushed home with maids, the way began
Left the palace, the King
Her journey started. Attendants followed

The delegation, let's go
Royal palace's slowly far
Came back near the Queen's home
A garden! Stopped! Then, all got in!

Lumbini[6]. It perfumed
Welcomed her birth, this term, the Queen
The lovely, pure garden
Large tree supported, event-ready

Smiled, held on branches
Blooming flowers then, she started
A baby was given
Birth - and this was so meaningful!

The dawning world, in turn
Happy joy, fresh passion fully
Kindness appeared every
Rainbow showed with many heavens

Extraordinarily!
Full moon, the date - only April
Opened, approached future
Kingdom, all the people, got news

Rest time was just refused
Group turned back due to the palace
The King, his servant's team
Welcomed them back with deals of love

Took place then, festivals
Full-on flags, jubilant dancers
The land - near, all over
Peaceful gladness - flower's fragrant

So that the newborn son
The King - Queen, with servants: his name...?
"Siddhartha[7]" means peaceful
"The one brings good, fortune, success!"

The prophet's visit

Signs, the Prince's birth-giving
Prophets guessed meanings, supposed:
Will have glorious years-old
Simply famous. There's no be doubted

A hermit who was known
Holy, respected. Exposed forest
The man's name: Asita[8]
Heard of the birth, though far, quickly

Palace - got, met baby
Silently looked, and he stood
Then, back. His face was full
Sadness! Gazed at now all the sky

The man started to cry
The King and Queen: surprised, also
Hurriedly asked the old:
"Any signs bad, on hold, teacher?"

The prophet answered:
"Worry? No need! Master, please!
A good physiognomy
Glorious beauties exposed

The future is grown
Brilliant, great, a whole genius!
Subordinate, if hold
Your land - will make the throne brightly

Be the King with glory
Peaceful fairness, happy people
A guru? Will prefer?
Leaving the court, discover - someday

The future shines its way
Beings, of course, all say: "Teacher!"
Noble benefactor
Open mind, not normal, come on!

Realize sadness' the world
Get out of the royal and go
Look for methods to show
Sufferings with pain: no longer!

Doctrine, in deep, gathered
Will teach this, whoever follows!"
Sadly, said, it's slow:
"My life has taken: old and time...

Not found the golden arms
Giving and help among pains, all
Sorry, caused not last long
To learn the truth, from...! Sadly!

Then, the Prince, just he
Point out the road's initiation
Till now, be better than
Much more famous, transcendent power!"

Lovely look at, after
The old man left, overseeing
So happy, just the King
Still hope: "What brings someday...

Kingdom, he would stay
Reigning a realm away and then
Till old, towards to, when
Concerns Buddhist - this man will be..."

The death of Queen Maya

A few days passed later
Maya died of severe illness
Before this leave, the Queen
She asked her sis, within a wish

Taking care of the Prince
The baby's days have seemed seven
"I promise." - She said
And, pleased to, it can, must be

Mahapajapati[9]
A surrogate - baby's mother
Time passed over, over
The Prince got older each day

The boy - the little sage
A kind, smart, grave angel
The King invited masters
Taught the boy, them: teachers, those days

Did well subjects always
Beyond instructors! Meant: superb!
Seven years old - starter
And then, good at literature by twelve

Thirteen years old, further
Martial arts did so well in all
Tradition, of course, comes
Imperial part's human before

The benevolent Prince

The royal palace's full
Of trees with birds, all animals
Surrounded the Prince - leader
The heart emitted his mercy, and

One day he walked alone
The garden looked, oh, falling swan
While flying. Though peaceful
Suddenly shot, a cruel arrow

Fell now next to flowers
The Prince's foot, inner - be ill
Hugged up the bird to feel
Mourned fully, checked to heal its wound

But looked via the garden
In a hurry, his cousin rushed in
His name's Devadatta[10]
Bow in hands with, from far, shouting:

"I shot that bird myself
Hope you give back to…, well, shooter!"
Disputed words - over
After, put a legal court on

To have correct judgments
Opinions were sudden: two ways
One side: "Who shot, who may…
Take the bird back, stay ever!"

Other: "Who stopped hunter…
saved the bird. The creature's his own!"
Dilemma! What a fault!
But then, a sage, in turn, appeared

Virtue, old age right here
Asked! All of the courtiers to try
The old man gave his mind:
"What a worth of this life, people!

So, the bird must be to
Who saved it with all truth of love
And shooter, that's evil
Far away, keep! Creatures: no harm!

Give bird to Siddhartha!"
Courtiers admitted. Encouraged mood
Reasonable! It's full
Obeyed all with the solved matter

Smiling with wonder
The King rushed his soldiers to invite
the old, whole palace to find
Nobody got, though tried. How strange!

The plowing ceremony

Remember, childhood here
Beginning of the year, at nine
Courtiers, the King, his child
At field - visited a while plowing

A new, succeeded season
People's enough, even much more
Intense sunshine, outdoors
Bustle in festivals. It's long

The King stepped deep field
He plowed for luck. To deal furrows
Farmers rushed down, followed
A season started, also, country

Let's go so happily
Plowed, waited to see seeds in
Watched, pondered - the Prince
He felt so many deep sympathies:

"Bullocks worked terribly
Peasants' whips hit anytime, and
Midday, full sweaty noon
Both all were wet, too soon over

The plow deep straight entered
Most insects with injured bodies
Survived? Immediately
Small birds pecked quickly as baits

And then big birds passed. They
Fell, found to take away small birds
Hunters in bushes lurked
Bowing to shoot big birds must die

Wild animals beside
Forest, to wait, to bite hunters."
Alas! Just food morsels
People and creatures were killed

How happy? Life to feel
Made soul of the Prince painful
Bored - he saw these scenes
Found: village road's shades in a rush

Under a tree, quietly
Meditated! And he thrilled
Sorrowed! The ditch, the field
Species fought until all died

Wished: the world would be fine
Sufferings with pains. Mind...? Never!

Beautiful lady Yasodhara[11]

The King expected the Prince
Grow up to be a skilled leader
But, him…, was too gentle
Calmly, quiet under flowers

Worried he will leave home
Succeed to the throne? Refuse!
The King called courtiers in
Meeting to look for mean methods

Opinion, the last turn:
"Let him with a royal time in!
Choose a wife just within
Beauty, so make the Prince enthuse

Passions of love must feel
Baby, their birth until later
Void dreams - no longer
Will like, and love much the throne!"

The King agreed at all
Quickly, urged officials to deal
Party! People got news
Welcomed ladies as beauty queens

Songs of music, lead-in
Many gifts - the Prince offered
Guests, in turn, went over
The last one was noble, pretty

The Princess, next country
King Suppabuddha[12], she's a daughter
Yasodhara. That's her
Beauty exceeded, better than all

She was so beautiful
The Prince made all fall in
Silently they stood, then
Suddenly gave her hands, please gift!

And he realized, until
On table had, within nothing!
He just took off his ring
Gave, as a gift - a thing engaged

Smiled - her happy face
Then she came back, stayed her sit
Love songs started again
People witnessed - rushed into the palace

Told the King as good news
Not long for that, he and mandarins
To the neighbor, met him
Suppabuddha to heal friendly

To propose, only
But that King said, immediately:
"Ask my Princess, you see...
Around here had many others

With my country's manners
People compete all together
Who wins the top: winner!
Take the Princess as traditions!"

Competition for wedding

Suddhodana thought through
The Prince's hard now to succeed
Confident words - the Prince
told the King, please let him relax

Time passed quickly, and then
Day designate, all men gathered
The Princess's over
On stands up - winner's reward

At first, shot with long-range
Many arrows, the same distances
Most people achieved goals
Central targets on all their turns

Also, a man, more than
Arrow pierced through, even, backside
Three layers, though tight
It was unique! So mighty! But

Although all were well-done
The Prince's face gave one smile
His pull, the bow, divided
He had to change the worthwhile one

In the King's palace, instant
Heavy, so hard, difficult to use
Calmly, his face was found
The Prince got right now the bow,

pulled it, made the arrow
Central target - flew so fast
Hit strong - it pierced in all
Seven layers of bronze easily

It's a great dowry
People admired. Plenty of cheers
The next, sword dance right here
The skilled sword could tear all things

Big tree, now it's pruning
Though trunk's so big, passing, all men
Next session - the Prince
Chose the biggest, immediately

Two trunks were grown closely
No one dared to…, but he. And then
Lightning so fast, as dreams
His sword now just passed in seconds

The tree stood, was firm
With hero - it's arrogant, teaser?
Suddenly, a gust's wind
Made trees fell down green grass, so

Be shocked, of course, the crowd
cheered up, with lots of shouts, pleasure
The third contest transferred
Riding a horse. Able men, well?

In the palace: the black, huge
horse was known much cruel. And so
People, horseback, let's go
But, were thrown, horse rolled up, down

Its hooves kicked back with chaos
Neck, mane all up, neighed out awful
The Prince, in his turn
"Honey wins wild. Control!", thought that

"Take gentle words, with love
Conquer nature of all species!"
Adjacent touch, and he
To horse ears with only sweet words

Rubbed head of the horse
Stroking the mane and fondled, then
The horse returned - a friend
Be meek. The horse's rampant? Not so,

climbed its back. Let's go
Riding it fast. Aroused cheers for
Applause: the horse's conquered -
celebrated him more. Great!

Next to the Princess, she fell
in love. Glancing instead of words

The pleasure palace

Later, in the palace
The King made just within pleasures
Ceremony's couple
Got married, this, ever came soon

Sixteen. So beautiful!
Twisted threads, mutual lovers
The King thought it over
"Keep the Prince in a gold cage!"

His courtiers, "Build...", were said
"...three palaces look majestic."
Fresh grass with trees
Sunny lotus, windy, lightly

Blue lake - white cloudy
The pair attracted many months, days
The first palace, always
Summer wind's cool - four ways: streams

The second one within
Winter's warm fires inflamed, flickered
The third palace, further
Rainy music's erotic days

Gardens with the kingdom
Covered all - most high walls outside
Sufferings - tried to hide
To come into their mind and souls

Musicians were proposed,
played well to grow a lull
Dancers - so beautiful
Voluptuous shape's full bodies

Sorghum smelt tasty
The Prince's made deeply in love
spent months, and his days
The joyful time to pave him all

Never saw or discerned
Misfortune with despondent lives

A new fresh song

Seasons withered, blossomed
Harmonious..., in one party
The Prince thought it deeply
At night, confused, only jumbled

To fall asleep better
He wanted music, middle tonight:
"Diva! I will require
A new song that not tried ever!"

All minds of the singer
Made him melt with mental soul, by
Heaven and earth were praised
Scenery with all nice beauty

Valley, forest, and sea
Luxurious streets, poetry's mountains
Desired? - Didn't confirm
But lands onwards he turned in mind

Golden palace! Outside?
So many scenes to find out. Then
The next day, he just went
After he asked for rambling

The King thought, "It's coming…
My son's warm with living the court
These all things, from was born
Country knowledge…, beyond to gain

Throne! Future, he will
Kingdom he rules, still gold's life!"
The King quickly obliged:
"Bring the Prince, outside travel!"

He met an old man

Wanted lots of good things
Tomorrow he's coming outside
Sorrows won't be defined
Sufferings in his mind: avoid!

The King ordered these points
Officials with kinds of people
"Decorate out, inner!"
Lanterns' streets, flowers' houses

Clear bad sceneries:
The poor and sick immediately
The morning, next, early
Channa[13] was said, and he drove

Wagon, horse Kanthaka[14]
Waiting by scenes: near, far, and strange
From childhood until
The Prince left within, the first!

Kapilavatthu[15]'s full
of poetic views all around
Roadside, people waited, shouted
To: see him was counted on dreams

spoke out a great deal
Of words to praise him - young King
of near future coming
Happy, he was! These things as songs

The city was gorgeous
Magnificent, prosperous
Suddenly a figure
An old man - bent, curved his back

The face's sad, on the wane
Thin body with skin: wrinkled
Stick-aided shamble
The Prince looked, with a frown

Asked. Channa said. It's caused:
"Years, a young man before..., time passed
Youth's not still at all
He becomes weak, in turn, old, sick

All of us face this scene
Old age invades within months, days
Slowly but always
makes you older, your fate's unchanged!"

The first time, something strange
Made the Prince maintain troubles
Frightened by that later
His soul's full of terrors. Oh, dear!

He told Channa to leave here
Back home now, just immediately
The heart murmured sincerely:
"Older, no one will be escaped!"

Met a sick person

Courtiers reported the King:
"The Prince's sad during these days"
The King heard. He amazed
Thought of a trip away from home

Kapilavatthu, once
This time, to suburban areas
Rapids, hills, lakes, rivers
Seductive shapes, erotic soul

Channa, the Prince, their go
A man: made them were noticed by
Just moaning, no smile
While the masses, in mind: cheerful!

"That person. He's wide-eyed,
coughing - his body vibrating
The face's pale, different?"
The Prince asked questions, Channa?

Kneeling, he said slowly
"It's a disease that is carrying
Today's healthy, smiling
Next days: sickness's turning painful

No one escapes at all
There are days: sick and fall ill. Sad!"
Listened. Be shocked, so then
Sorrows, the Prince's heart's plenty of

No more an excursion
He told Channa - instant: back, now!
Sadness! It's all around
Royal favorites died out. No more

The son's sad. The King saw
So, he rushed to call for courtiers
Let's discuss all ideas
To find methods to cheer him up

Requests of everyone:
"Stop: go on a jaunt alone!
Next time, it's suburban
Included music, royal dancers

With some the officials
Visit parks with able fun games
So awesome. It will charm
Flowers, birds among the sky."

Met a death

The third trip was designed
Procession. It's like royal
A strange scene. By his own
The Prince saw - alone, simple:

"A group of sad people
Small steps on the field's trail
Taking a coffin away
Inside: a person. And they're crying"

Pointed Channa, that thing
And he asked him, surprisingly:
"People! Tragically!
Who's that, inner? Tell me, where to?"

Channa, on knees, and told:
"Relatives, too sorrowfully…
for him, who died must be
Friends included, what a pity!"

And then Channa, clearly
What the palace buried. His say:
"Person, who passed away…
Likes us! On his birthday, he's born

Then, kids grew up. Small
Seasons went past to turn: the youth
Pleasures enjoyed, are full
Or life: sickness, loss constantly

Floating lives. Maybe
Glory took! Infamy held!
Old age invaded piecemeal
Body - spirit must feel depressed

One day, full of sickness
Lay on the bed, within, waiting
for days: breathless! Away
No one escapes this day, never!"

Wasn't seen, heard - ever
"Birth, age, sick, death"… further, by days
Made the Prince hesitate
Thinking in heart: "Images, no far…

Beautiful child, bride
Friends, fame with rights, and throne
The body, yes, it's all
It's durable - No, don't be fixed

It's fascinated, charming
People sink with passions, sex, and
Forget! It's near the death
Forget the flimsiness of life!"

Pleasure faded

Beautiful views garden
Streams babbled, quickened branches
The Prince's wagon came. He's
welcomed by songs with rhythm's sky

Parties were organized
Tuneful dance, sound, with lithe people
And smiles? No, never!
The Prince showed trouble with thoughts

About scenes of sorrow
The funeral! It's so impressed
Short life - impermanent
All fun! It's just momentary

Courtiers gathered closely
Enticed to make him: be happy!
But, he immediately
Said: "This scene is captivating

Exciting festivals
I also want a role to play
But thought it, - It's always:
That charm escapes all faded circles...?

Fun, all will be over
Impermanence - numbers of kinds
Pain is released - my mind
How to? Fun? No! - Till find that path

River, full of pleasure
Seduce me? Hard to the wrong way!"
They knew the Prince's soul's pale
To the palace, so they returned

Heard. The King's sad. And all
night, stayed up late, revolved his mind

The idea to leave worldly things

Time then went with the wind
The Prince's joy - it seemed boring
Now abnormal eating
Pale, thin, worn as hanging by threads

One day, his father: met
Pessimism, and then, was shown
Let him, please: his go
Blue? One more to know the sky

Relieved soul, heart, and mind
With confusion - held tight inside
The King's so satisfied
Asked the courtiers: be silently

Followed the Prince, and he
Must have the trip celebrated
Village with scene felt strange
Country's wide, fresh. Nice fields were green

Riding his horse alone
He paused by vast farmlands to feel
His soul spread. Not seemed
to hear fun jokes near him, courtiers'

Under the sun, and he
Walked, watched farmers, to see plowing
And, all of a sudden
He saw boundless golden lights, from

A person - his dress's worn
The shirt's tattered, whole - all the same
But, the face was gentle
Holding a vase. Leisure's going

Clean, courtly beard, hair
Outwardly - meek, deliberate
He asked: "Hey, who are you?"
Stopped. Answered - the Taoist calmly:

"Wandered all the mountains
and the forests. Religion - search for
Not family. Be sure:
To find the truth. All were ignored

Looking forward saving
People get off dark scenes, sadness!
Fake life's impermanent
First - raises, late - sets, as dew - the same!

This money, with that fame
Can you bring all - leaving the earth?
Keep off all sins of greed
Also, your lust, deep love, desire

Leave the circles of life
"Birth, age, sickness, death" by each day
I try to find a way
People's release - help they arrive!"

Finished, he turned away
It seemed to inspire this day, event
The Prince's sublimated
Thought silently: "The way, have found

Homeless! Here, must leave, now
Beings will get morals from me!"
The mind's so strong, as aim
Back to the court, waited for the King

Counting on submission
Good news, the birth - event of him
Time went by with dreams
The first child of the Princess, now

Listened. The Prince confirmed:
"More obstacle for me, oh dear!
Add thing binding only
Escape this place! Immediately!"

"Binding wire" - good motion
Name of the child, nascent way, so
"Binding wire" - Rahula[16]
The court's satisfied, his father's too

The plan that came true
Held the Prince - a golden cage

The King's worry

He wanted to find the light
One solemn day, the Prince submitted:
"With all respect, father
Always, I wish with a passion

Leave the palace, these things
Become a monk, non-home, go far
Pray to find over
A way to end sufferings, yes!"

The King heard his request
With fear, for a long time, came true!
Choking, he answered to:
"Small, don't leave, don't lose... please

Here, rules our country
Till old, not late - the disclaimer!"
He said: "No, it's never
You don't help me, father, such things

Escape all sufferings
Escape circles: aging with time
Escape sickness that harms
Escape the death. It can't be changed!"

The King heard and screamed:
"What you're thinking, it's meaningless!"
Determinedly, the Prince:
"Keep me closely. Will it be good?

I'm here, as a jailbird
Let me get off, my turn, please!"
The King said angrily:
"The citadel must be besieged

Bring guards, carefully
Keep the Prince must be inside!"

Beyond the truth

Leaving the King's palace
The Prince's soul within one thing:
Leave home for religion!
So his palace - events and fun

Although so beautiful
There was no charm engaged with him
One night after the feast
It seemed a miracle appeared

Dance troupe and safeguard team
All were tired. All seemed asleep
Yasodhara within
Holding baby warmly in bed

He looked at his wife, child
The Prince's heart can't hide his mind:
"Although love much parents
Beautiful wife, my son included

But I decided became
A monk only - the aim: find bliss
Methods to free all species
This pleasure life, this is worthless!"

Parting! Hugged the baby?
Afraid: woke up, so he didn't
Lightly then he walked there
Climbed the window and carefully

Followed the long porch roof,
got down to the ground, and he
Found Channa, said: "Right now…
I just want to go out tonight

The horse, prepare for me!"
The servant was very surprised
was woken at midnight
However, he's all right executed

The horse's rubbed by the Prince:
"Hey, Kanthaka, I mean: let's go!
Silently, people so
Asleep. You make me go out, though

Kapilavatthu's nice
Keep me here, no. Oh, I must leave
This grave night, you see!"
The horse's silent, seemingly like-minded

Followed: Channa at night
Brought the Prince - goodbye kingdom
Under the moon, a while
Riding, he looked back wide palace

Prayed: "Way! Just the time
Sufferings end. I, then come back!"
Galloping all night till
Brightened sky. Came in forest

It was quiet all, and
Moral monks gathered can be seen
February, the eighth within
Twenty-nine years, it meant: passion!

The Prince's just feeling:
"It's time to seek religion. Begin!
Channa, hey, not pensive
Bring back Kanthaka immediately!"

Channa cried. Not believe
That the Prince left. Now, he has gone
Sympathetically:
"Thanks to my loyalist, Channa

Once I leave home, you see
Body's full of jewelry? No need!
Bring back to the palace
Meet my father, and kneel, say that:

I go with no anger
Leaving home - love father and home
Because of him and all
I'm on my path. I turned away

Liberation - it may
Be found then I'll stay at home
Whatever, take a fault?
My King must leave. Also, I die

Also, this paradise
Natural death, no fight against!"
He took the sword, within
A cut-up made until his hair

Parted. Gave back, Channa
watched the Prince walk out of sight
Sad horse, slowly backed all night
To the palace. Details reports:

The Prince left the King
Farewell - he made to silk royals

The beginning of the morals' search

Musical songs' chorus
Welcomed him - Siddhartha, go on!
Luxury clothes, it's all
not suited for this: a homeless monk

Met a hunter with fun
Siddhartha made a done exchange:
Rough pants, clothes within
Simple outfit. Soul: meaningful

Waded streams, climbed up all hills
Looked for teachers - morals to study
Everyone met him, only
Thought him: "Different, considerable

The person's face is bright
Evangelize, help life's future."
Samana[17] in these days
Met teachers, satisfied? May not!

Not like his constant wish
Thought: far away! It needed to travel
He knew that Magadha[18]
The kingdom had the propagandist

So - rushed to look, and he
came to Rajgir[19] city, once day
The palace was beautiful
Officials saw: informed the King

"There's a poor Taoist
But looks like superior, holy
The steady face, figure
The golden light on the body!"

The King treated, hastily
To him, with talks to see real life
The King Bimbisāra[20]
Listened to him - near, far stories

Admired, he said to him:
"Besides you, yes, you will be loved
Please stay here, this way
Help me rule it, nice days' country!"

Replied, refused, hurriedly:
"The Great King, please know me - the monk
Ever gave up my crown
To travel, to find. Count on, master!"

The King heard with joined hands:
"Wish you good luck, be on your way
Find out the truth someday
Please help this place, people

Although success or not
Please come back, the more. I wish!"

Six years of fighting

His journey: leisurely
took him to a lovely forest!
Many people here, and
He's fun with these brilliant teachers

Teachers named: Alara[21]
Willing to teach: Uddaka[22] included
A short time just passed soon
Understood all words of them

Not satisfied, his thoughts
"Must cultivate alone, myself
Find the ultimate truth!"
He went on a further journey

Niranjana[23] then be
crossed. And brought he: the forest
It's near the holy land
And he met five ascetic monks

Five brothers, Kaundinya[24]
Their method: tormented bodies
Said: "People who live, ever...
The more you pet, the closer it pains

Now, force bodies strictly
Sufferings: lose, immediately!"
Listened logically
Asceticism, then he practiced

Painful legs, back, body
Too cold winters, hottest summers
Sitting whole days. Little
eating, sleepless, haggard-looking!

All nights, awake. Feeling
Body of dust, looking skinny
Time passed, six years! And he
Thought: the day of renunciation

Away from home's event:
twenty-nine's age added six years
Thirty-five now, at here
Enlightenment - don't realize, oh!

Before, in the kingdom
Pleasures with all things surrounded
That wasted life was found
Then, a place to count on, yes!

High mountains with deep caves
Painful of self-cultivation
But, what was the result?
Both lives: first, next - mistaken things!

The goal of true living
Middle way's path to think: follow
Eat and drink every day
The body, mind - all may be pure

Meditation. It was
He got things now, be sure, clearly
Samana trailed lightly,
had a bath in a river's waves

Dust, dirt's taken away
Weakly, onshore, he stayed to rest

Offerings

There's a cowherd family
Lived in a small village next to
the forest. Name: Sujata[25]
Her newborn son - all are healthy

Pleased with her wishes
So, she brought milk into the forest
Thanksgiving! Worshipped the Gods
Going, she saw gradually

Image of Siddhartha
At tree shadow, from far, distinguished
Although thin, weak. Still
bright. She thought: "You mean the God

Sitting here reigns forest!"
She offered milk in front of him,
opened his eyes, within
joyful. Slowly drank milk, smiled, thanked

Milk made his health better
Samana said: "Offering, yes…!
It's precious, so well
Not a God - I'm human. Being

The noble truth! Seeking
Misery's stopped. Helping people!"
Seeing now, Siddhartha
Bathed, ate, drank all, not as a monk

Five brothers, Kaundinya
Discussed, decided: went far the forest
came to Banares[26] and then
In Sarnath[27] park: ascetic monks

In the forest stayed
Samana had his way, alone

The great fight

Crossed river towards,
for far. A place to meditate
Met a person with grass
Samana asked. Lined for sitting

Smooth shady tree, and
Welcomed, Bodhi[28] branch nearby
What a great worthwhile!
Quiet desert, the sky's clear

Fate's support - created right here
The monk, under the green tree. And
Facing East, he sat down
Hands-on the feet's soles then, promised

to himself, he made, was
"Even I have to die, this place
Never! Don't leave! It means
Never give up until - get goals!"

The devas so rejoiced
April full moon made by today
Ancient legends were said
Evil - bad forces always, there are

Often harass our minds:
"Greed, anger - inside, ignorance
Jealous, with suspicion."
Guilty things in making friends

Horrible acts and then
Caused by sad moods, enhanced troubles
Demon Lord - it was called
Demon Lord made its full stop

Samana was disturbed
With terrific storms surrounded
Violent winds spread out
But the Bodhi tree found peaceful

Meditation's powerful
So, the landscape it's all unharmed
These ghosts and those devils
Used poison with archery. Shot

But the arrow flew to
turned into wings of lotus. So
Demons changed their approach:
turned into sexy girls, flirting

Twisted soft bodies, dancing
Royal pleasure, now bringing back
The monk still meditated
Demons were hard to face, so then

The Demon Lord failed down
Try for the last! Just found methods
Alone appeared, uttered
words, as dissuaded, as ridiculed:

"Hey! The great Prince
You thought better all mean people
Twenty-nine years, ever
Enjoy yourself in the palace

Six years of tormenting
Thin body, weak - practicing, useful?
Meditation of fool
Miracle's hard, not soon to get

Who is your witness? Soon
Religious life's successful others?"
The Demon Lord mocked
Easy to shake the believer - his mind?

Samana - his right hand
Pointed to the ground and then touched down:
"This world - the witness, now!"
Correct! It changed how many lives

When men, women live - die
Reincarnate. It finds poor, rich
Tolerance, patience, loving
Get ways to help sufferings - people

The Demon Lord - failure
forced it to leave. As a nightmare!
Alone, relieved right here
The monk, bright moon, cleared - the sky

A fragrant spice. It's nice
The world must be sublimed, ready!

Awake

Samana Siddhartha
Now - meditated on far-thinking
Quickly, profound wisdom
Realized past and even before

This life, when it's over
Then next life - another follows
Death is physical ruin!
Then, new bodies are soon reborn

He knew everything created, all
Every caused by human beings
They sowed - effect: getting
happy or sufferings, many lives

He knew each - all lifetime
Correlated, lived among others
Deep truth's brainpower
Saw things - miraculous, around

Sun, stars, planets - all now
Meditation helped, found galaxy
Recognized things. It is
from a dusted piece to a star

Always, things change. They are:
Birth. Be killed. Birth - reincarnation!
Then corrupted, generating
Everything has its things: in causes

He realized all the world
Sufferings with afflictions are full
Lusted pleasures, they, so
Never: pains' source? - Don't know, never!

Things are temporary
Not know! So find only to harm
To expect, satisfy
Evil pursuit's desire, so much!

But the profit - fame earned
Don't bring happiness for us, long time
Circle of slip, then still
Why did to search to deal with these?

Resentment with hatred
No sowing peace! Melancholy!
Miraculous! It is
The way human misery ends

Be enlightened, like him
Stop desires immediately
Always filled things lovely
Song's roads to peace, happiness, yes!

Samana Siddhartha
He knew in whole the above reasons
It's melted: dark's ignorance
Halo: body suddenly filled

Normal person? Not him!
Be enlightened. Achieved the goal
Beings' Buddha has been
His pure smile with peace's body

Buddha's Enlightenment
Dawn's then bright, pink-coated nature
Sun, in the East, appeared
Sun shined brightly - down here, all fields

Welcomed Buddha Shakya
Mountains' flowers - all nice, fragrant
Near, far things: exciting!
Melodiousness! Chirping, the birds

The clouds spread: radiance
Colored rainbow: accented the sky
It's beautiful, so fine
Everywhere stunned. Surprised people

Choose persons to teach morals

Great source of endless fun
Dark's ignorance becomes dispelled
At Bodhi tree, his turn
Buddha thought of pleasance. Days, months

About happiness, which one
The root of it has done - taken
But he thought it lamented
Hard for beings to cultivate

So, hide here by myself
Enjoy peace source, be felt alone
Suddenly his mind called:
"Suffering world…! You consider...?

We longed for it ever
Please, teach us, get the morals!"
Buddha heard in his heart:
"The way find truth's full of thorns here

Long-term efforts, persistence
Lots of energy, people follow?"
In mind echoed the soul:
"We are in darkness. It falls through

But we now don't delude
People can take this truth, many!"
Buddha hesitated - now he
Previous images appeared

The lotus in a lagoon
Flooded trees are difficult to rise
But others passed, otherwise
Reaching high with its shined petals

Also, some trees worse
Floating on all surface sides
Beings are so defined
Many people were dived. In maze

Couldn't! To get, away
From the dark, it may be hard
Many people made fast
to have a berth - last practice's find

By sun, lotus blooming
Far from mud. Reaching water
Priority, higher
Initiate strugglers, their way

As lotus, it's rising
Enlighten this religion, be felt
Smiled Buddha: "Good! Well
Of course, I will show, tell human

Cultivates - ends sufferings
Enlightened with helping people
But you must remember
In life, first, administer yourself

Which Buddha saves you, well?
Beings do it themselves first!
Listen: great morals
Before relying on Buddha

Whoever comes, they are
enthusiastic, try hard to learn
Sincerely with morale
Happy to teach, obtain gold truth!"

Buddha thought at first, to
Instill someone, teach who's quickly
Thinking before, at once
Years of hard work had done and passed

With teachers: Alara
And Uddaka, the past taught him
But they now passed away
He then thought of five ascetics

Kaundinya, brothers
Strictly practiced, ever with him
At Sarnath park, now in
Near Banares - sacred heaven

"I seek to teach first, them!"
Buddha went in urgent to preach

The first teaching

Buddha walked slowly
Through camps with villages in days
Gentle, tall, and grave
Made countryside always peaceful

Though poor or rich both all
Buddha treasured equally then
Equal love without ends
As rain watered all fields, lakes, ponds

Sarnath park was pink on
Welcomed Buddha to stop his steps
But five monks whispered, then:
"Should not embrace this man truly

Samana's left, so he's
not ascetic. Worthless in mind!"
But when Buddha's nearby
He's majestic: realized, appeared

They all stood up right here
With their respect immediately:
"Welcome to Siddhartha
It is so good - you are back now

Study here with our -
asceticism - just found old days!"
Buddha thanked, gave his say
"Understand me, please... you all

I'm now are different
Siddhartha - no, it won't be called
Unsuitable - that name!"
Five people asked, "What name? You are?"

"Look there…" then said - Buddha
"Worldly beings fall asleep
Ignorance's infinite
Now I awake them - this dark life

Forever, the truth: find
Call Buddha, yes, enlightened people!"
With devotion, inner
All five monks just uttered: "Please,

Buddha, my respect! You
give us the way to feel releases
The golden truth's preached
Enlightened life, quickly as you!"

Four noble truths[29]

With five people's requests
Accepted. Buddha made then: sermons
"The dharma wheel's motion"
Moved "Wheel of dharma"'s[30] event, has found

"Dharma" is a high truth
Buddha said that - "it's too, this life
Four wonderful truths, right
"Four noble truths" - must mind, people!

Four great things. It's the
way to help us to struggle dulling:
- One: it's called "Suffering."
Suffering's truth. It warns about

Unfortunate life, now
"Birth, age, sick, death" are found all days
Hunting pleasure, always
At last, the gash got, maybe! Poor!

Whether satisfied, sure
Look, in the end, it was nothing
Never satisfying
Hard to have peace. Being happy

- "Origin of…", two is
"… Suffering" life, only the cause
Our minds contain this, so
A lot of lust, years old's greed

Suffering comes with ease
Like people have many gold stores
Devote it. Share...? Ignored!
A poor life! Caused: craved - for much wealth

Tangled thoughts - long day fell
Made trouble for oneself to feel
"Cessation of suffering"
- Three. End fast such things, the root

When we clean our minds
Eliminate lust - fight greed
Suffering stops. We will
be peace, and extremely happy

- Four, next: "Path to…", further
"… Cessation of suffering", yes!
Let us now shake off pains
"Middle Way" path between extremes

One: to enjoy the world
Passionate lust constantly. And
Two: be ascetical
Mortifies with whole, own bodies

The noble eightfold path[31]

Middle Way's beautiful
The eight-legged path is all relieved
"Noble eightfold path" soon...
Reach Enlightenment, Nirvana quickly

The path, with eight legs, is
Surely take us - immense light:
"Fairly accept things' core
Think more and speak it honestly

Always do things clearly
Fraud, theft, kill must be got out
Don't to dishonest fields
Diligently, goodwill: follows

Keep minds clear and so
True things to think with no: forget!
Sustainable thoughts, on
Brightly makes wisdom shining."

"Noble eightfold path's" things
Happiness with ending sorrows!
After listening, so
All five monks! All follow together

Realized extreme - the truth
Please, disciples into…, by him
Five ones, first. Confidence!
Persuade that path. Religion, follow!

Prayed for Buddha, how
to get the way, to know the shore

Bright golden religion

Then, Golden Religion
Followed Buddha, instant to life
The earth liked dawn, beside
Buddha preached with high passions

Ways: finding. Words: choosing
To children with helping adults
Buddha brought it at ease
Finding methods quickly to show

People with much know-how
Buddha fully dissociated
Someone's taught piano
Quiet and not: to show a word

But those great sermons
Set a shining, noble-minded life
Buddha's kindhearted, so fine
Compassion brimmed, bright moral

Crazy, stupid people
were taught, Buddha's patience towards
Quickly spread morals
Many dear disciples followed

Friendly male, female
Praise Dharma. Buddha's loved, cheered
At home or left, all here
People practiced so earnestly

No class of their own
As Buddha said: "Sea's all rivers!
Big and small, over
Into the sea, rivers are merged

Salty: before, after
With the same name, color: oceans!"

Praise

One day, someone praised:
"The Great World! Amazingly!
This rare old master is"
Buddha heard, said: "Don't be, this life:

Wasted energy's praise
Only respect? And try: belief?
Just do it by yourself
Bring my words, practice - then?

Seeing that right: believe! -
believed it, so thanks to Dharma!"
Buddha's modest, as far
Across a river, Dharma: a raft

A finger to the moon
Pointed out the truth, way - all follow
Of course, rafts, if it so
Many kinds - rivers - overcome

Pointing finger, the moon
Of course, many, and all pointing
In search of lasting truth
Many paths, not secluded, my own!"

Then he said more: "Beings!
This life must have great things, people
Many priests everywhere
Many methods to share - help lives

Don't disparage in mind
Take care of tasks to raise your own!"

Sermons at Veluvana[32]

Time went by fast in turn
One day, Buddha remembered: him
The King, Bimbisara
The kingdom of Magadha waited

Visited, he returned
Took disciples, settled on hills
By days, sermons - helped life
The King, people - heard kind, true words

People, near-far, in all
Refuged Buddha, be full of joy
A few people, the King
Then gave Buddha offering: a place

Veluvana garden
Among city, sermons to share
People heard great morals
Buddha's name - be wider - near, far

Devadatta

The younger brother
His name, Devadatta: envied…
Find more bad links, and he
Harmed Buddha - no hesitation!

Buddha at the cliff, in once
Meditating. But run rumble
Above, evil people
Pushing rock, each other - they tried

Fortunately, it's kind!
Rolled away sides. He's fine, peaceful
Once Buddha took his turn,
visited Rajgir, the golden city

Disciples came with him
Bad people knew, told each other
Fed elephant, got drunk
Used trees to beat, elephant annoyed

So, it's crazy with chaos
They then released it out the road
Buddha, passing by. Then
Hoped elephant killed men - all monks

People were feared and run
Except: Buddha, he's untroubled
Showed love - included mercy
Elephant felt immensely

Out of rampage, madness
Slowly walked, knelt freely, and
Buddha rubbed its head, then
Taught disciples: "Good can be well

Hatred? Not ends itself
But ends with all immense kindness!"
Later, things happened - meant
Devadatta got, for him, mischance

Before dying, within
Apologies, so sincerely
Prayed to meet Buddha
But caused by bad karma, before

No way for him - not saw!
Died! Fell to hell with tortures. So
Causal law made himself
In many next lives. Well, badly!

Coming home

One day Buddha was on
the way back to his hometown, at
Kapilavatthu's well
Prepared this for all lavished

Welcomed him - Buddha's feet
Followed, a group of disciples
Everyone with their cheer:
"The Prince - beloved, now here's the Master

The Master's so noble
Opens - the capital - its arms!"
Suddhodana is proud:
"What a great, right now, honors!"

The King's anxious, his heart
Many years waited his turn back, then
Servants, horses, he sent
To check: strange for anything

Courtiers, so, rode horses
The next day backed, and he said that:
"Buddha and disciples
Mornings with bowls - beggars for food!"

The King heard - angry mood:
"Become a beggar? Royal son here?
Affront, it made, oh dear
Must be stopped immediately!"

The King was led quickly
To see Buddha and he realized
His son, a gentle child
Became Buddha with high thoughts now

Shining bright around
Disciples - they sat down courtly
The King asked. He thrilled
"Too poor? Humbled yourself for food?"

Buddha: "Not difficult
That's a thing as custom, followed!"
The King's angrily, so
Shouted: "Don't say shallow things, please

The royal family
Gold tray, silver cup. Be this, so why?
Custom to beg, it's right?"
Buddha listened - politely said:

"Dear father, yes, long since
Your ancestors, all mean the Kings!
But I practice, help life
Follow lineage - that kind, Buddha

Humble, get alms every day
The Master made. Obeyed custom!"
Held his father's hands! Then
Buddha walked - spoke so tenderly

Taught the King miracle
Showed how to end suffering's life
After Dharma, it's fine
All of the pearls, so kind in words

The joy came back - the King
Then praised: "You're getting so far!
Supreme priest, you are
Noble Master of family

I salute. Accept me
A disciple. Here is a joy!"
Buddha's time lived, stayed
His wife and son, all they're earnest

The wife - Yasodhara
With the son, Rahula requested
Take refuge, learn Dharma
Be disciples. Buddha accepted

Buddha accepted more then
The gentle old stepmother
Shakya lineage, later
All, be his disciples. So fun!

Bourgeois man - Anathapindika[33]

A few days, his hometown
Buddhism's path went now, again
Shravasti[34]. He just came
There was a man, his name with fame

Anathapindika
Long time, admired Buddha. He then
Own gold, silver - spent
Buying gardens. Intended: buildings

will be built for using
Monasteries. Beings were preached
Here, Buddha with sermons
Sutras teaching, "Giving!" he stated:

"Offer Buddha and monks
Good! But not as taking refuge
Buddha, Dharma, Sangha[35]
Good! But not as forcing oneself

Keep five precepts. But, well
Better, your mind is melted in love
With compassion, kindness
Sentient beings' merit, the first:

is to develop, all
Intellectual wisdom, to know
No: permanence. It's so
Impermanence! Here's how: There - Gone."

King Suddhodana's death

After preaching, years
The news noted his King was ill. So,
Buddha then took his go,
returned home met his old father

Seeing sad, wilted father
Buddha preached Dharma beside
The King's relieved his mind
Peaceful Buddhist chant died with him

Bhikkhuni[36]

The King had passed away
Women - be nuns - so they wanted
At first, Yasodhara
Then, the aunt - Buddha's mother

Asked to be Bhikkhuni
Buddha stated: practice something
"Eight Laws" they must follow
Between males and females, two groups

After that, Buddha went
Worldwide. Time: he spent - helped life

Forty - five years of Dharma preaching

Enlightened, thirty-five
years old. He went to mind the world
People woke by sermons
Cities - villages set foot with him

Buddha - an example
Dawned of wisdom, brighter mercy
Alone sooner, later
Also, disciples - closer beside

All years - months, he just tried
Buddhism's path was widened, but
Three months: rainy season
Disciples, him - resting inside

temple, they settled down
Stayed, preached throughout the season
Buddhists, all now coming
Gathered, on listening: Dharma

Offered monks and Buddha
Raced to learn - each other - they did
Buddha's voice's powerful
Rhythm's lion, ocean tides' sound

The final days

Buddha taught Ananda[37]:
"My age, eighties. It's far, so, and
Everything's done now, then
Helped people with wisdom, mercy

Go now! I am ready
To pass away, no regret, yes!
Listen, hey, carefully!
It's the goodness of religion

Just like a wish, it will
Four types of disciples. Enough!
Bhikkhus[38] with Bhikkhunis
Upasaka[39], Upasika[40] obeyed

Helped me preach good faith
"Wheel of dharma" to lay on life
My body's weak and tired
Ever took it! With my last time

Dharma wheel went on far
Impermanent! The car's worn
Now: want to back, just home
Kapilavatthu all for last

Then I will pass, this place
The citadel - old days, I lived!"
Buddha's words said to him
Ananda's sad voice - it seemed in tears

"All my heart, The Great World
Please, don't leave the road - middle
You go, just merciful
Your disciples - return? No way!"

"Why: cried?" Buddha said
"It's all certain for death, the true
Live, die - these things merge to
Impermanence, you lose my words?

And, when I leave this world
Engrave Dharma with all your mind
My words! Practice - must try
Instead of me. It's kind gurus

Show ways across the shore
Enlightenment's just for waiting
No need me - no, nothing
Let's get ready: coming home now!"

Buddha, disciples, out
Went to the North, more thousands: miles
Stop at Kushinagar[41]
A small village not far from home

Disciples, next Buddha
Rest in the shade: village garden
Buddha told Ananda:
"Extinction's place, nirvana, yes!"

The final disciple

Suddenly, an old man
Subhadra[42] - the villager came
To meet Buddha, a chance
Buddha agreed against tiredness

The old man's utterance
Religious life turned. In troubles!
Sincerely, Buddha taught
After that, he was all happy

Even end days, it is
Buddha always saves depression
The old man was pleasant
To take refuge so earnestly

He wanted: leave home, please!
Buddha accepted, as he: Sangha
The earth's shining near, far
Golden lights - the final disciple

The final instructions

Buddha, then leisurely
In a hammock, now he's lying
Between two Sal trees[43], bring
all white flowers, blooming: welcomed!

Surrounded by disciples
Only a few people crying
Otherwise, unspeaking
Minds: pure! - Watched him, kept things quiet

Buddha's voice was gentle
The final words, passionately:
"Children, remember me:
my words I taught for many years

It's lust! It's greed! My dears
The cause of so much tearful pain
Impermanence! Life changes
Don't be greedy! No anything!

Practice, make efforts. When
Purified mind - bodies then get
rid of your life. Obtain
Eternal happy fame, glory!"

He stopped. Taught again:
"Light up - own torch, to change your way
Dharma I taught today
Use as a torch - the maze to leave

Enlightened shore within
Only yourself! Not in others!
Children, don't be waiters
Long for release? With others? No!"

Buddha entered Nirvana

Buddha, after - advice,
turned his body, the right, gently
His head's set on - now, this:
the right hand, with mercy in eyes

Eyelids closed. All right!
Peacefully passed, his mind, away
Nirvana, now obeyed
Entered! Out, Sal petals' shedding

Covered this sweet garden
Lunar April, event: full moon
High sky, moon's shadow, all
Tonight, shined as golden lights now

Shakyamuni's body
Respectfully, burial's well
Later, seven days then
Was moved to a large temple, for

Cremation as form
The custom - this old long land. But
The fire burned - not be on,
waited for his disciples. Till

Knelt in front of the coffin
Then, all flared instantly, fired
A time passed, it subsided
After burning whole, finally

Exposed ash bones, could see
The precious relics of him!

Dividing relics for worship

Eight countries around here
In the North of India. Old days
The Kings all: took away
relics. Sharing? It may be fought!

Finally: - Had a sage
Gave his advice detailed, valid:
"Almost all life, with him
Buddha taught us. It seemed one thing

Do not hate! Be loving!
Aggressive! Following his words?
Nirvana - has just turned
What a cruel betrayal, oh dear!

Stop arguments here
Equally, let's, these relics, do!
Hold back: to build temples
Worship relics, after as now

Grateful to Buddha! Found
Wisdom's teacher, abundant love!"
The advice's good and sound
All Kings agreed. They now obeyed

The Dharma still exists

Buddha now passed away
India, since that. It may be far
Two thousand more extra
Five hundred years. Buddha's teachings

Still: our hearts' meaning
Abundant love - wisdom was full
Beyond time, borders, so
Generations followed, handed down

The faith, who keeps, just now
Goes to the light, joys: count upon
Suffering? Want to end?
Quickly carry out to Buddha's

Hatred, selfishness, greed
Exterminated! It's now all done
Teachings of compassion
Liberation, nothing worried

Illume magic wisdom
Body, mind as peaceful Buddha
Follow his path, not far
Sentient beings: Buddhas will be

Great Enlightenment:
brings peace to a shining life!
For all sentient beings
Always happy - all things - near, far!

Shakyamuni Buddha
His full words in the verse. Simple:
"Evil? No, it's never
Do good deeds with those who wait, hope

Keep the mind must be kind
The Buddha's words, let's try to do!"

Notes

[1]. Himalayas: a mountain range in Asia. It has some of the planet's highest peaks, including the highest, Mount Everest.

[2]. India: a country in South Asia. Its border: the south is the Indian Ocean, the southwest is the Arabian Sea, and the southeast is the Bay of Bengal. On the land border, it shares the west with Pakistan. The North with China, Nepal, and Bhutan. The East with Bangladesh and Myanmar.

[3]. Maya: the mother of Gautama Buddha; she was the wife of Raja Shuddhodana (the father of Gautama Buddha).

[4]. Suddhodana: leader of the Shakya (were a clan of Iron age India (1st millennium BCE), inhabiting an area in Greater Magadha, situated in present-day southern Nepal and northern India, near the Himalayas), the capital is Kapilavastu. He was the father of Siddhartha Gautama, who later became the Buddha.

[5]. Shakya: Shakyas formed an independent oligarchic republican state known as Sakya Ganarajya. Its capital was Kapilavastu, which may have been located either in present-day Tilaurakot, Nepal, or present-day Piprahwa, India.

[6]. Lumbini: a garden - a Buddhist pilgrimage site in the Rupandehi District of Lumbini Province in Nepal. Here Queen Maya gave birth to Siddhartha Gautama around 563 BCE. He achieved Enlightenment sometime around 528 BCE, became the Buddha, and founded Buddhism.

[7]. Siddhartha: Gautama Buddha, popularly known as the Buddha (or Buddha Shakyamuni). He was an ascetic, a religious leader, and a teacher who

lived in ancient India. He is the founder of the world religion of Buddhism.

[8]. Asita: a hermit ascetic. He was a teacher and advisor of Suddhodana. He predicted that prince Siddhartha of Kapilavastu would become a great Chakravarti (the secular counterpart of a Buddha).

[9]. Mahapajapati: was the Buddha's foster mother, stepmother, and maternal aunt (mother's sister). She was the first "Bhikkhuni" (Buddhist nun).

[10]. Devadatta: a cousin. He is the brother-in-law of Gautama Siddhartha.

[11]. Yasodhara: the wife of Prince Siddhartha - the mother of Rahula and the sister of Devadatta. Yasodhara became a Buddhist nun and is considered an "Arahata" (or Lady Arhat).

[12]. Suppabuddha: was the maternal uncle and father-in-law of the Buddha.

[13]. Channa: a royal servant, a head charioteer of Prince Siddhartha. He became a disciple of the Buddha and achieved an Arhat later

[14]. Kanthaka: a favorite white horse with eighteen cubits of length - a royal servant of Prince Siddhartha. Siddhartha used Kanthaka in all major events before his renunciation of the world.

[15]. Kapilavatthu: an ancient city that was the capital of the clan of the Shakyas in ancient India, where King Suddhodana, Queen Maya, and Prince Siddartha Gautama lived until the Prince left the palace at the age of 29.

[16]. Rahula: was the only son of Siddhartha and his wife - Princess Yasodhara.

[17]. Samana: is a term that existed before the advent of Buddhism. Many religions use this term to refer to those who have renounced the secular life. Thus, Samana is a general name for monastic goods in ancient India, including Buddhism.

[18]. Magadha: a region and one of the sixteen "Mahajanapadas" (a set of sixteen kingdoms that existed in ancient India), 'Great Kingdoms' of the Second Urbanization (600-200 BCE) in what is now south Bihar (before expansion) at the eastern Ganges Plain.

[19]. Rajgir: Its meaning is "The City of Kings." It is a historic town in the Nalanda district in Bihar, India. It was the first capital of the ancient kingdom of Magadha.

[20]. Bimbisara: was the King of the kingdom of Magadha at the age of 15 and was the first King to meet Buddha Shakyamuni. He became a Buddha's disciple. He gave Buddha and the Sangha his Veluvana monastery as offerings.

[21]. Alara: a hermit and a teacher of ancient meditation - the first teacher of Gautama Buddha.

[22]. Uddaka: was a sage and teacher of meditation identified by the Buddhist tradition as one of the teachers of Gautama Buddha.

[23]. Niranjana: a river that flows through the Chatra and Gaya districts in the Indian states of Jharkhand and Bihar.

[24]. Kaundinya: was known as one of the first five Buddhist monks. He was the first disciple of Gautama Buddha and became an Arhat later.

[25]. Sujata: is a farmer's wife. She fed Gautama Buddha a bowl of "Kheera" - a milk-rice pudding, ending his six years of asceticism. The gift gave him enough strength to cultivate the Middle Path, develop meditation under a Bodhi tree, and become the Buddha.

[26]. Banares: was Varanasi later. It is a city on the Ganges river in northern India. Varanasi was officially revived after 1947, but the city is still widely known by its earlier name: Benares. It is located in

the middle Ganges valley in the southeastern part of the state of Uttar Pradesh.

[27]. Sarnath: is a city in the state of Uttar Pradesh, East India, 13 km northeast of Varanasi. Gautama Buddha first taught the Dharma in Deer Park in Sarnath.

[28]. Bodhi: the Bodhi Tree - "tree of awakening" - is a large sacred fig tree located in Bodh Gaya, Bihar, India. Siddhartha Gautama attained Enlightenment about 500 BCE under it. In religious iconography, the Bodhi Tree is recognizable by its heart-shaped leaves.

[29]. Four noble truths: "the truths of the Noble Ones" - the truths or realities for the "spiritually worthy ones." The truths are:

1. Suffering: the truth about this life. It is an innate quality when existing in reincarnation. It is not only unpleasant sensations that are suffering. Suffering refers to all physical and mental phenomena. The law of change and decay controlled them. So all the happy things are also suffering because they will perish. Life is a set of sufferings.

2. Origin of suffering: the truth (origin, arising, or "cause") and the reality of suffering come with craving. While craving is traditionally translated in western languages as the cause' of suffering, it can also be seen as the factor that forces us into suffering, or as a response to suffering, trying to get out of it.

3. Cessation of suffering: the truth of cessation (cessation, confinement) suffering can be ended or prevented by removing or severing ties with craving. The fact of giving up the claim will release the bondage of anguish.

4. Path to cessation of suffering: The Noble Truth (Eightfold Path) is the path leading to renunciation, the end of craving and suffering.

[30]. Wheel of Dharma: a widespread symbol used in Buddhism. It remains a major, significant symbol of the Buddhist religion today.

[31]. Noble Eightfold Path: the path of Buddhist practices leading to liberation from samsara, the painful cycle of rebirth, in the form of Nirvana. It contains:
right view, right thought, right speech, right action, right livelihood, right effort, right mindfulness, and right concentration.

[32]. Veluvana: in Shravasti (see 34), Veluvana (Bamboo Garden) and Jetavana (Yellow Garden) were the first two monasteries where Shakyamuni Buddha taught the Dharma. Nowadays, this is an important pilgrimage site for Buddhists.

[33]. Anathapindika: was the wealthiest merchant and banker in Savatthi in the time of Gautama Buddha. He was the chief male patron of the Buddha. Anathapindika founded the Jetavana Monastery in Savatthi, considered one of the two most important temples in the time of the historical Buddha.

[34]. Shravasti: the capital of the ancient Indian kingdom of Kosala - where the Buddha lived most after his Enlightenment - is one of Buddhism's most revered sites. Here the Buddha taught many of his sermons.

[35]. Sangha: bhikkhunis (see 36) and bhikkhus (see 38) live by the Vinaya, a set of rules. Male and female monastics are members of the Sangha (Buddhist community).

[36]. Bhikkhuni: see 38.

[37]. Ananda: was one of the most loved figures in Buddhism. He was known for his memory, erudition, and compassion.

[38]. Bhikkhu/ Bhikkhuni: is a fully ordained male/ female monastic in Buddhism who lives by the Vinaya, a set of rules.

[39]. Upasaka: see 40.

[40]. Upasika is used for women, and Upasaka (39) is used for men. They are not monks or nuns. They undertook certain vows before that. They are devotees, followers who stay at home, not in pagodas.

[41]. Kushinagar: a town of the Kushinagar district in Uttar Pradesh, India, where Buddhists believed Buddha attained "Mahaparinirvana" (nirvana-after-death). It is an international Buddhist pilgrimage center.

[42]. Subhadra: the name of the last disciple who took refuge with the Buddha. He was a Brahmin. He went to meet when the Buddha was about to pass away, so he left home and attained Enlightenment.

[43]. Sal tree: Sala tree (scientific name: Shorea robusta) is a species of flowering plant in the family Oils. Legend states that Queen Maya gave birth to Gautama Buddha under a Sala tree in Lumbini garden, Nepal.

THE FOUR NOBLE TRUTHS

    1. Life: is suffering.
    2. Cause of suffering: is selfish desire.
    3. Ending desire: will end suffering.
    4. The eightfold path: will result in ending desire and attaining enlightenment.

THE EIGHTFOLD PATH TO ENLIGHTENMENT

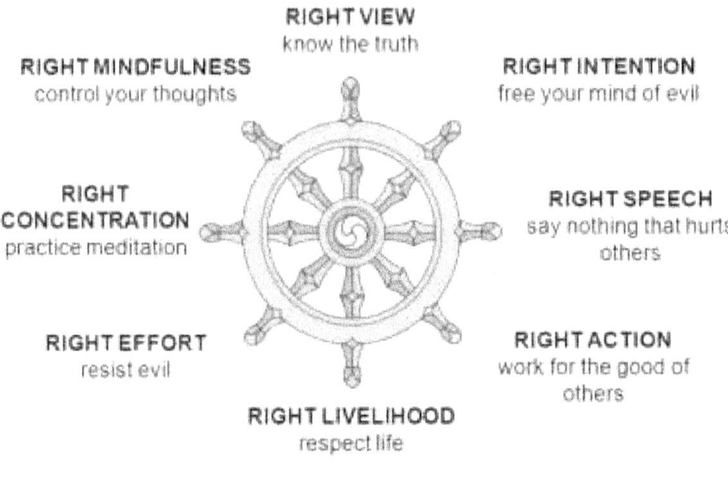

****

AFTERWORD

Which Buddha saves you, well?
Beings do it themselves first!
Listen: great morals
Before relying on Buddha

ABOUT THE AUTHOR

VAN QUANG PHAM

This book is my first one that finished with all my love and effort. I hope to receive much from you to improve my writing for this heartfelt life.

I would like to get your opinions at quangpv.hd@gmail.com

Thank you indeed!